Wreaths for All Seasons

TEXT AND PHOTOGRAPHS BY
Steve Sherman

THE STEPHEN GREENE PRESS
LEXINGTON, MASSACHUSETTS

First published in 1986 by The Stephen Greene Press, Inc.
Published simultaneously in Canada by Penguin Books Canada Limited
Distributed by Viking Penguin Inc., 40 West 23rd Street, New York, NY
10010.

*Photographs on pages 82–83 are by Glen Sherman. Used by permission of
the photographer.*

Text design by Joyce C. Weston
Production by Unicorn Production Services, Inc.
Printed in the United States of America
by Winthrop Printing Co., Inc.
Set in Trump Mediaeval and Windsor Light Condensed
by DEKR Corporation

Library of Congress Cataloging-in-Publication Data

Sherman, Steve
    Wreaths for all seasons.

    Includes index.
    1. Wreaths. I. Title.
SB449.5.W74S48   1986   745.92′6   86-9777

ISBN 0-8289-0586-X

Acknowledgments

*Thank you for your good advice and help —
Barbara Bowen; Deborra Doscher; Ann Geisel;
Lillian Harrigan; Mary Hibbard; Steve Palmer;
Janet and Dick Quinn; my mother, Genevieve
Sherman; my brother, Glen Sherman; and as
always, Julia Older.*

Contents

Acknowledgments **v**

Introduction **ix**

1 The Meaning behind Wreaths **1**

2 When and Where to Display Wreaths **5**

3 Tools and Materials **8**

4 Dried-Flower Wreaths **10**

5 Evergreen and Cone Wreaths **34**

6 Cloth Wreaths **70**

7 Grapevine Wreaths and Door Decorations **84**

8 Edible Wreaths **102**

Supplies **113**

Index **114**

Introduction

Although I include simple directions accompanied by photographs here to make the basic styles of wreaths, this is a book of suggestions. Please use it as a jumping point to your own imagination and designs in making wreaths.

Looking repeatedly at something that you want to copy sometimes sparks a flash of an idea for an alternative, a slight twist that makes it in the end more personally interesting, more satisfying to you since you put some of yourself into it. The same goes for these wreaths. They can ignite your fancy to try something different, and be all the more fun because of this.

Nearly all the wreaths presented here were made by the people at whose homes they were photographed. The wreaths are offered as a gallery of examples. Some are simple, others complex; some traditional, others radically unusual; but they all can be made by hand at home. The possibilities certainly don't stop here. They're endless — different materials, different designs, different sizes.

As you'll see and enjoy, making wreaths takes small effort for such giant reward.

Wreaths for All Seasons

The Meaning behind Wreaths

The beauty of wreaths includes their symbolism. The display of wreaths to represent special meanings has been traced to the earliest civilizations. Archaeologists found remains of rings of flowers and sprigs 4,500 years old in the burial pyramid of King Sekemket in Egypt. On the lid of the king's sarcophagus lay such a wreath, which according to the Egyptian *Book of the Dead* signified that the king had performed good works during his life and that the wreath, as a symbolic eternal circle, was a sign of eternal life for him as a reward. The Egyptian word *ankh*, in fact, means both "wreath" and "life."

Wreath headdresses of silver beech leaves with gold pendants of willow leaves and beads of lapis lazuli were found in a large grave of Sumerian women, apparently buried with religious ceremony. These remains also dated 4,500 years old.

Throughout history wreaths have been associated with life, rejuvenation, renewal, fertility, fecundity, the eternal seasons borne forever of themselves. This is the reason that wreaths were made from plants, which as organic life formed into a never-ending ring linked a person to everlasting life.

Unlike simple branches or bouquets, wreaths easily could be displayed in many places without changing their form. They could be worn on the head, placed on a coffin, hung on a horse's neck, attached to a building, fashioned around a pillar (which symbolized the course of the heavenly bodies around the sun).

Many ancient customs were associated with wreaths. Those who gathered the fruits at the end of the harvest season and who performed the Jewish Feast of the Tabernacle traditionally wore wreaths. Wearing wreaths on the head was described by the Latin word *corona*, meaning both "wreath" and "crown."

Eventually, wreaths were divided into two general types. *Corona convivialis* represented happiness, good fortune, and triumph. These wreaths, for example, were placed on the winners of sporting and literary games, as well as on military conquerors. *Corona funebris* represented death and mourning; these were positioned on coffins and tombs and carved on gravestones.

Bridal wreaths combined both types. Representing virginity and the new married life to come, wreaths of flowers woven into a circle were set upon a bride's head as a wreath of happiness. At the same time, the wreath as a sign of mourning represented the dying of the old life of the bride and the beginning of the new.

Many cultures used wreaths during the everyday life of their peoples, especially young women about to marry. In Arabic countries, brides wore wreaths of orange blossoms as signs of fertility and marriage. In China wreaths made of olive leaves signified success and achievement in the literary arts.

The ancient Greek and Roman cultures used wreaths extensively. In Greece both the bride and groom and all the wedding guests wore wreaths. The ingredients of the wreath varied according to what the marrying couple wished to emphasize. To dedicate the marriage ceremony to Hera, the goddess of marriage, wreaths of quince were worn. If to Hymen, god of weddings, marjoram wreaths were made. Myrtle was associated with Aphrodite, the goddess of love.

When children came of the marriage, wreaths were hung on house doors in Athens. An olive wreath told friends and neighbors that a boy had been born. A woolen fillet — a little band or ribbon for the hair — made into a wreath meant a girl.

When the children grew up, they may have entered the games held in various parts of Greece. Winners would be crowned with certain wreaths, and all others would know at which games they had triumphed. Victors in the Olympic Games, held in Olympia, received wreaths of wild olive leaves. Those in the Isthmian Games in Corinth received pine wreaths, while winners at the Nemean Games in Nemea were crowned with parsley wreaths. Champions at the Pythian Games in Delphi were bestowed with wreaths of laurel, which were dedicated to Apollo — god of the sun and the creative arts. Since the games included contests of poetry and dissertation, laurel wreaths over time became associated with the arts, scholarship, and creativity.

When the Romans absorbed much of the glory of Greece, they included laurel wreaths to honor victorious generals. The Roman emperors wore wreaths of roses, but it was the laurel wreaths that held distinction for superior individuals in many fields of endeavor, not merely on the battlefield.

In the military, generals were not the only ones to receive the honor of wreaths. Ordinary soldiers who risked their own lives to save others were awarded the highest honor — a wreath of oak leaves. When such a soldier wore the wreath and entered an amphitheater, the entire audience rose in honor and respect. An oak wreath became known as recognition of bravery, patriotism, self-sacrifice.

Eventually, wreaths of plant leaves evolved into wreaths made of jewels and "leaves" of gold. These became the crowns of rulers. In one of the far corners of the Roman Empire, the established wreath of gold became the crown of thorns that the Roman soldiers used to ridicule Jesus, "King of the Jews."

Down through the ages, wreaths continued to be part of the cere-
monial functions of peoples. The Church finally absorbed the tradition
of wreathing champions and special people. These "wreaths" were the
halos given Christ, the Virgin Mary, and the saints and martyrs in
frescoes, paintings, and illuminated manuscripts.

Advent wreaths originated in the Lutheran tradition and showed
joyous anticipation of Christmas. In churches, evergreen wreaths with
four candles were lighted one at a time for the four Sundays before
Christmas as a symbol of the light to come. These Advent wreaths
were also set on dining tables in homes. Elaborate della Robbia wreaths
included hand-painted, enameled terra-cotta objects first made by the
della Robbia family of fifteenth-century Italy.

Yet the wreath as crown continued. In 1804 Napoleon crowned
himself with a wreath of gold laurel leaves.

Today wreaths remain as symbols of honor, distinction, patriotism,
bravery, special achievement. Crowns of royalty persist in the modern
world, and so do the wreaths of olive leaves, which symbolized peace
in the ancient world. The symbol of the United Nations, for example,
is the planet Earth encircled by a wreath of olive leaves.

Oak wreaths are seen today on military insignia, badges, and other
decorations. Funerals still display wreaths of sorrow; tombstones are
still engraved with wreaths. Winners at horse races are bedecked with
wreaths of roses. Brides still wear wreaths of flowers.

Whatever the origin of wreaths and their symbolism, each individual wreath can be more than a reference to something else. It can be a
colorful ring of cones and nuts, a balsam evergreen emitting a tantaliz-
ing forest aroma, dried summer flowers brightening a long winter, vivid
patterned cloth, fall leaves and Indian corn, ribbons and roses. Ancient,
meaningful symbols enrich our lives by joining us with our past, but
above all, wreaths can give us beauty here and now.

When and Where to Display Wreaths

Depending on the types of materials you use, wreaths can last years. The use of dried flowers, for example, has lengthened the time to display wreaths. In fact, this particular kind of wreath can decorate a home throughout the year and, if cared for, last for many years — giving simple, full pleasure season after season.

Colors in dried-flower wreaths are a welcome treat during long, dark winter months, especially when flowers from home gardens lie dormant and flowers from florists become more expensive. To see vivid reds and oranges, blues and violets in January and February brightens your spirits as well as your front doors and living room walls. And if your wreath is made of fragrant herbs, such as sage and rosemary, then you enjoy an extra dimension.

Evergreen wreaths remind us in winter (when we most need to remember) that green spring and summer are not gone forever but only waiting ahead. As with the dried-flower wreaths, evergreen wreaths have their special aromas, especially if they're made with balsam branches. The sweet, lush forest smell of balsam adds a rich fragrance to a home when chilly north winds are blowing outside. It's another help to lead us through the darkness.

Cone wreaths and cloth wreaths last longer than both the dried-flower and evergreen ones. These can be displayed the year round for years at a time. If they're properly placed and protected, they'll hardly show their age.

When to Display

Traditionally, Christmas wreaths have been evergreen wreaths, and Thanksgiving has been the day when they are first hung on the front door or over the fireplace mantle. Usually, they're kept up through the holiday season and, along with the Christmas tree, are taken down a few days after New Year's Day.

Nowadays, however, wreaths have become such a welcoming sign of life and hospitality that more families are leaving them up for months after the New Year. Wreaths are also being used to celebrate Easter in spring as a symbol of renewal and the true new year — the resurrection in the cycle of life and death.

Where to Display

The front door is the long-standing favorite place to display a wreath. Everyone can see and enjoy it there. Not only do family members delight in it every day, as do visitors on their arrival, but also strangers passing down the street can appreciate it. Displaying wreaths on a front door is a comforting gesture of openness and good cheer within.

Depending on the traffic, however, dried flower and evergreen wreaths on doors sometimes get worn and torn. So be judicious in deciding on the spot to hang them. Remember, too, that wreaths between a front door and a storm door can get squashed or, if located on the south side, can get "cooked" by the sun's heating up the space between the two doors.

Other places besides the traditional front door are appropriate. For example, wreaths can be hung easily on the inside of a living room bay window, which frames them strikingly from the outside.

Try placing a small wreath in surprising, out-of-the-ordinary places. A miniature wreath on a back door would dress up what is always considered a cheerless, utilitarian entrance.

If you have a curb light on a pole, a wreath there would draw the eye and spark the spirit. You might wire a string of tiny outside lights to the wreath so that it could gleam at night.

Backyard patios are natural sites for hanging wreaths. Nail them to arbor posts, near an outside lamp, or on the outside house wall. If you have a tree at the back line of your yard, hang one there so that you and guests see a winsome wreath in the distance as you linger through the summertime.

Don't forget the garage door. Tack a wreath there at both top and bottom, so that it fits snugly when you open and close the door.

A wreath centered on a family room chimney is always a comforting sight to see. Small herb wreaths hung in the kitchen are in their natural element, and, of course, wreaths used as centerpieces on dining room tables are attractive and appropriate.

The possibilities are open-ended — bedroom walls, at the end of hallways, at the top of stairs, high on the crowning point of your house roof, the back of your fence.

Tools and Materials

You need only basic tools to make wreaths. Except for an electric glue gun, the tools are simple and inexpensive. Of course, applying glue by hand can eliminate the need for a glue gun, if, in fact, glue is needed in the first place for a particular wreath.

You probably already have most of the tools in your household garage or workshop. But whatever you don't have at home can be found at a nearby hardware store or home center.

The materials are inexpensive and can also be found either at home or a nearby store. Yarn shops, craft stores, cloth outlets, sewing centers, low-cost department stores have what you need if your attic doesn't provide you with old woolens and cloth or your backyard with pine-cones and branches. Some stores sell "seconds," or slightly flawed materials, which are ideal for making wreaths. The felt wreath on page 83 is an example of using less-than-perfect material to make a wreath with unapparent flaws.

A florist shop can provide you with tape and coated wire as well as balsam branches, fresh flowers, silk flowers, and other appropriate ingredients. A craft shop is a prime source for the straw and metal ring forms on which to build your wreath. Some wreaths actually need only a reshaped wire clothes hanger.

The following list includes tools and implements that you might use. You certainly don't need all of them for any particular style of wreath. Most likely, the wreaths that you'll make will require only a few items. Nevertheless, this list gives you an idea of how basic the necessities for wreath-making are:

heavy-duty scissors
pliers
floral or hair spray
green florist tape
metal ring
hammer

glue
stickpins
thread and needle
pocketknife
pencil compass

coated wire (20 and 22 gauge)
wire cutter
paintbrush
hooks for hanging
sewing machine

Again, the following list of materials is intended to give you an idea of the simplicity of possible materials and how readily available they are:

dried flowers
cones
seedpods
patterned cloth
grapevines
dried field grasses

reed mats
spray paint
nuts in the shell
ribbons
felt

plastic fruits
plastic flowers
evergreen branches
candy
polyester fiber

Dried-Flower Wreaths

Wreathmakers say that they've never made any two wreaths the same. Ultimately, every wreath is a singular, individual creation because of the innumerable detailed differences in similar plants and their flowers. Two wreaths may be close to being identical, but a closer look always reveals that they are truly unique.

Although every wreath is different, basic underlying principles have evolved from making wreaths that can help newcomers to the art. Here are some to keep in mind:

- a finished wreath is usually four to eight inches larger than the base mold
- working continually on a flat surface is deceiving, so periodically put the wreath on a wall for a better perspective (the corollary to this is never buy a wreath having looked at it only on a table or counter)
- Spanish moss as a background base plant must be fumigated before use
- for a wide wreath, overlap the flower and plant bunches at an angle; for a thick wreath, pile the bunches on top of the base and each other

- if you want a particular color to stand out, work with that color first
- after your base is made, divide the wreath into an odd number (say three or five) of sections; then work on the decorative part (this way the wreath doesn't end up too obviously symmetrical)
- place a tying wire or tape sufficiently away from a blossom so that the flower won't break or droop
- leave no part of the base mold showing
- use a variety of shapes of flowers to give depth
- never judge your wreath until it's done; being discouraged with how it is progressing and then throwing it away may waste a perfectly good effort
- if a finished wreath on the wall doesn't appear symmetrical, simply turn it a little and sometimes the wreath will straighten out to your eye.

Bases

The base is the foundation for your wreath. The most popular bases include:

green multiwire forms	straw circles	grapevines
single-wire rings	flat hemp	Styrofoam

Made in the shape of a deep channel, the wire forms or double-ring molds are designed to hold whatever background material you wish to insert. These forms can hold the material without tying it, although wrapping the material to the mold adds further sturdiness.

The single-ring mold is used to wrap and secure the base plant in place. Since it is a single ring, smaller and narrower wreaths can be made easily on these.

Straw bases are popular, especially if you don't grow your own base plants, such as artemisia, which is probably the most used background plant. With a loosely packed straw base, sometimes you can stick strong-stemmed plants and flowers directly into the base; but for a more secure fastening, attach them with a large U-shaped pin.

The woven hemp bases are good for the flatish wreaths. Gluing the plants to this is the usual practice.

Grapevines harvested during the fall are ropelike and flexible. They are used extensively, especially in combination with the bright orange–colored bittersweet plant. The vines can be formed into circles to any desired thickness, tied down, and then decorated with whatever other objects you wish.

Styrofoam molds are light, inexpensive, and can be used particularly well with pins for securing stems and other items.

Drying Flowers

Most flowers are best harvested for drying when they are relatively young and their colors are vivid. The basic method is to gather a handy size bunch of stems together, gently tie them with kitchen string, and hang them upside down. They can be hooked carefully onto coat hangers, which in turn are hung onto pieces of wood or pipe fitted high in a dry back room or attic.

Hanging flowers upside down is necessary to protect the blossoms. If hung rightside up, the blossoms are apt to droop, possibly breaking the stem.

Depending on the size and type of flower, the plants may dry in from two to four weeks.

Silica gel, a desiccant, can also be used to dry flowers and to speed the preparation time. The gel is a grainy compound and normally used for the more delicate flowers, such as fairy roses, pansies, and violets.

Place some silica gel in the bottom of a baking pan, put the blossoms on top, and then spoon on more gel to cover the blossoms completely. The gel absorbs moisture from the blossoms and takes about five or six days to dry small flowers.

Silica gel can be mixed with cornmeal in a half-and-half ratio to stretch the supply. The gel can be reused time and again.

Plants to Use

The base molds can be covered with a number of sturdy, pleasing plants for the background, but the most popular and useful are:

silver king artemisia	silver queen artemisia
Spanish moss	sage
dried scented geraniums	lemon balm
Roman wormwood	tarragon
southernwood	santolina

The decorative part of the wreath can include any number of plants and their flowers. Your choice depends on the color, shape, and size that you would like to combine.

Here are some possibilities:

dried alfalfa	thyme	lavender
iris pods	coronation gold	parsley
milkweed pods	chive blossoms	sage
bee balm	eucalyptus	oregano
tansy	daffodils	bittersweet
cockscomb	yarrow	goldenrod
larkspur	rosebuds	columbine seeds
mums	statice	love-in-a-mist
bachelor's button	asters	Chinese lanterns
baby's breath	rose hips	sweet basil

Beginning

A benefit of herbal wreaths is their fragrance. They can fill a home with pleasing smells. (If you use santolina, which is a moth preventative, it can save your wool as well.) The more fragrance you put into a wreath at the beginning, the better in the end because some of the fragrance eventually will fade while some plants may overpower others.

For a strong fragrant base, you might start with southernwood, which has a very pungent aroma, and then add Roman wormwood, which is from the large artemisia family. Scented geraniums also exude a long-lasting fragrance.

The artemisia family of plants (illus. 1) provides one of the best arrays of colors and textures for background bases. Silver king artemisia, for instance, dries to a soft gray color and is pliable and strong enough to shape onto double- or single-ring molds.

Silver king artemisia, with the broad leaves at the bottom of the stem, and silver queen artemisia are two very useful background plants. If you grow them yourself, pick them about three-quarters into the growing season. Otherwise, they'll turn yellow later. They're easy to grow and prolific once you get past the three years it takes to grow

1

2

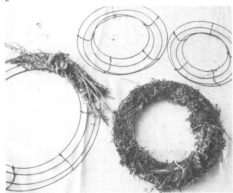

them from seed to harvestable size. You can buy mature plants instead.

As a point of reference, a large (say twenty-nine-inch) wreath uses about six generous bunches of artemisia.

Double-ring molds come in different sizes (illus. 2). They are shaped with one side open, into which you place your base plants. Usually, the plants are tied to the inside of the mold with florist wire by wrapping the wire completely around the ring and the plants.

Since the ring molds are green and artemisia is gray, either green- or gray-coated wire can be used. A well-made wreath has neither the ring nor the wrapping wire showing — a reason that you would not want to use bright red wrapping wire.

To make the base in a double-ring mold, place a bunch of artemisia into the mold, bending and shaping the plants gently as you go (illus. 3). The size of the bunch depends on the size of the mold.

For a single-ring mold, Spanish moss works well. Shape the moss around the single-ring frame (illus. 4) and secure with coated wire. Be sure to use fumigated Spanish moss that has been prepared commercially. If you gather the moss yourself from trees, you'll be in lots of bug trouble.

15

Using Simple Tools

You can make an attractive wreath with the simplest of tools (illus. 5). Heavy-duty craft thread can be substituted for florist wire. A roll of ordinary household green tape can be used to hold the stems of the decorative plants you plan to use. A combination wire cutter and clamp is handy for cutting and pulling thread or wire into place. Deep U-shaped pins can hold down a thick grouping of stems.

These pins can be used on plants to cover a straw mold (illus. 6), which is available ready-made at nursery and craft stores. Shape artemisia around the outside of the mold and pin the background plants securely in place. Begin with the inside of the ring. Continue doing the same until the entire straw mold inside and out is covered. Afterward, wrap the artemisia with the thread for a further hold, although this is generally not necessary.

Green plastic or cloth tape may be used to gather the stems of flowers together in bunches (illus. 7). This is done for the decorations once the background plants are in place. Be gentle with the plants as you work; they're fragile and can break easily. Tape them only enough to hold a bunch loosely.

5

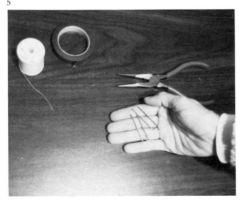

6

Once the flowers are taped, then they can be pinned or glued to the mold, depending on whether it's hemp or wire. For a flat hemp mold, gluing is better. Any standard glue will work. If you plan to make many wreaths, consider the purchase of an electric glue gun (illus. 8), which is less messy. Cartridges of glue are inserted into the barrel, and then you press a trigger to hot-glue the plants; the glue dries faster using this method, too.

Laying Out the Design

After the base mold is covered with the background plants, such as silver king artemisia, then figure your design and how you wish to emphasize the pattern of colors and textures. An effective way of laying out the design is to mark locations on the wreath where you wish to place certain bunches of plants.

To do this, take pins and stick them lightly into the wreath, leaving the pins upright and visible (illus. 9). This shows you where to begin each grouping. Odd numbers in patterns on wreaths seem to work better for the eye than an even number. In other words, stick three or five pins into the base wreath as your guides.

7   8

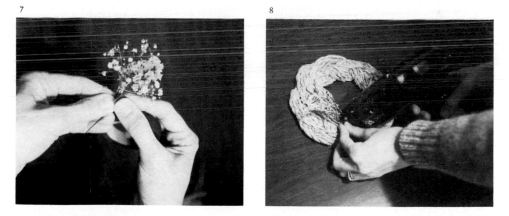

9

Then prepare your bunches of flowers and branches, attaching them to the wreath at the guide points. This method keeps the spaces between the bunches equal. Be sure to include the same kinds of flowers and branches in each bunch to reinforce the pattern.

As you progress around the wreath, hold the wreath up at eye level or hang it periodically on a wall to examine from a vertical perspective. Working only on a horizontal table may distort the symmetry you're trying to achieve.

If your wreath is likely to be close to people coming and going who possibly will be touching it, consider spraying it with an aerosol can of clear floral spray or hair spray. This helps to strengthen the fragile materials.

10

General guidelines and rules are important to follow in that they save you experimental time by borrowing on what others have discovered already. On the other hand, breaking some of the rules can produce appealing results.

For example, you could simply not proceed beyond covering a straw base mold with artemisia (illus. 10). Instead of creating a traditionally decorated wreath in a full-circle symmetry in patterns of three or five or more bunches, try a single bunch. Dried grasses arranged in a spray with a few silver king artemisia and tied with a bright ribbon at the center make an eye-catching wreath.

If you grow and dry your own flowers, you'll want to set a space apart in your home for them. The space can be anything from a spare corner in an attic to an entire room devoted to nothing but dried flowers and making wreaths.

To dry most flowers, hang them upside down. Otherwise, their blossoms tend to droop and break off the stem. Drying the more delicate flowers by silica gel has been discussed earlier.

Tie a few stems together and hook the flowers over metal clothes hangers. Then hook the hangers over a string or pole.

The drying process takes from two to three weeks — maybe longer — depending on the flower and weather conditions.

Once the flowers are dry and rigid, they may be stacked upright in narrow baskets or boxes.

Virtually any flower may be dried and used to make wreaths. Experiment. Whatever you grow in your garden, try drying it.

Some of the flowers shown here include the reddish globe amaranth, which also comes in white and purple; ammobium everlastings (the small, single, white blossoms); yellow ageratum; physalis Chinese lanterns (bright red globes); pinkish acrocliniums; and silver king artemisia.

The startling simplicity of this wreath shows what can be done with a careful hand, a good eye for line, and a sense of how an understated series of muted colors works. The swirl of the silver artemisia gives the wreath vitality and motion. The slight angle outward of the artemisia is maintained throughout the wreath and gives it breadth and bulk — perfect for this winter door on a farmhouse built in 1784.

Achillea are the predominant gold-colored blossoms. This flower comes in different shades and is best picked when bright yellow. It's better to let this flower grow a little into the season, but not too long or the blossom will fade.

This wreath is made on a double-ring frame.

23

In contrast to the previous wreath, this one produces a startling effect through its complexity. Although its bulk is larger, its width is about the same. It's obviously designed to arrest the eye with a rush of color and texture.

At first glance, pattern appears lost to bold colors, but another look reveals what the maker did. The same left-to-right movement as in the previous example is built into the wreath, causing the eye to move this direction and to give the circle a "whirl" that underscores the liveliness of the colors.

The colors have patterns, too, but with so many textures included, seeing a pattern is postponed in favor of the sculptured "feel" of the wreath.

Its major flowers include the gold achillea, the cloverlike white globe amaranth, the spindly eucalyptus and delphinium, goldenrod, and grasses.

This small-scale wreath is appealing for its use of earth colors and textural symmetry. It's also an example of mixing the right color of Chinese (sometimes called Japanese) lantern with straw flowers, here the rust-orange blossoms.

Chinese lanterns are the papery, hollow globes that are greenish when they first appear — the stage of the Chinese lantern used here. A later growing stage turns the "lantern" a bright red-orange (see page 33). Placing the reddish straw flowers next to the red stage of the Chinese lantern would have unbalanced this wreath.

Straw flowers come also in shades of yellow, red, and white. Other flowers included in this wreath are the small white ammobium and statice along with silver king artemisia.

A deft use of deep rich colors, such as some of the delphiniums or sweet William blossoms, can enliven plain silver king artemisia backgrounds.

Try to keep colors within the same tone range. A few dark colors work well together, as in this example, just as a blend of a few light colors would. Deep blues, reds, and golds can be found among the pansies, petunias, and achillea yarrow, which is among the easiest of all flowers to grow.

A wreath can take many turns from being flashy to showing sophistication. This is more an example of the latter style because of its subdued aesthetics and mastery of technique.

*In this case, the shape conveys a mes-
sage. This Valentine wreath could be displayed throughout the year. It makes you
smile to look at it anytime.*

*The white gypsophila baby's breath are
so delicate that they go with nearly any
combination of flowers and can be used to
good effect in any size wreath. Instead of
purple oregano blossoms, you could choose
a small red blossom to fit the traditional
heart and Valentine color.*

Different size flowers of the same color are another option in building a wreath. These straw flowers (including the white ones) present a strong front of red, but the different sizes and textures soften the tone so that it doesn't become a solid red front.

This is a good lesson in plunging into a direction that may at first seem one to avoid. See what you come up with.

The pattern here is also unusual. The white blossoms are placed to divide the wreath into a top and bottom. At the same time, they are placed subtly enough to give the eye two views — a wreath divided straight across the middle while also unified by the full circle of reds.

Other subtle touches include the soft points of yellow blossoms scattered throughout the wreath, giving it another dimension that the eye may be slow to detect but that is nevertheless important. If you removed those yellow points, you'd find that you would want to put them back.

The Chinese lanterns in this wreath are an example of the late stage of growth from the greenish color when they first appear.

Evergreen and Cone Wreaths

Wreaths made with evergreen needle branches are the ones considered most traditional. The short-needle spruces and firs are the favorite tree sources, although the long-needle pines sometimes are used to good effect.

Balsam fir has long been chosen by people in the outdoors for spreading under their tent and sleeping bags as a fragrant ground cover. Of the 25 million or so Christmas trees cut every year, a third of them are balsam firs. They're popular for good reason.

The continuing fragrance of a balsam fir makes it ideal for wreaths. Balsams are easy to work with; their short, blunt needles with a white line underneath are firm and uniform; and they have lasting strength.

Preparing the Evergreens

As with the dried-flower wreaths, you need a solid base on which to fasten the evergreen branches. Use a single-ring frame. The large size well over twelve inches is better to accommodate the width of the branches so that your circle ends up with a space in the center, not a solid mass of green. All the tools you need for these wreaths are coated green florist wire and a wire cutter, which can do double duty to cut the branches from the limbs (illus. 11).

Cut individual eight- to ten-inch-long twigs from the branches

11

12

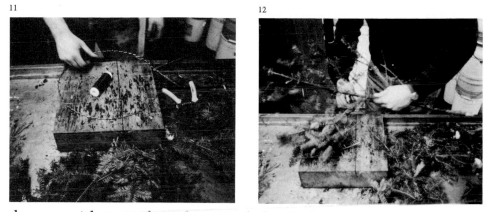

that you either purchase from a wholesale florist or craft supplier, or cut from your own woods (illus. 12).

Gather a handful of these twigs with the stem part together, layering one on top of the other (illus. 13).

Place them on the ring mold with one hand and wrap the wire around them with the other several times (illus. 14). Twist the wire ends together to secure and cut the wire.

Continue this process front and back of the ring until you complete

13

14

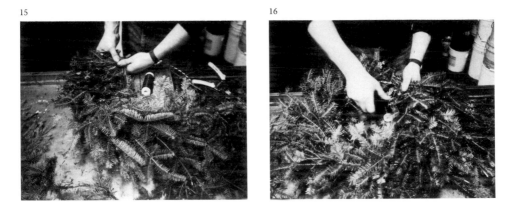

15   16

the circle (illus. 15 and 16). You can determine the fullness, size, line of motion, and symmetry of the wreath by the way you layer the twigs over each other. Angling the bunches more outward results in a "spray" type of wreath. Compacting the bunches gives you a thicker, neater wreath.

Cone Wreaths

Cones can be added to an evergreen wreath or a wreath can be made entirely of cones. They come in all sizes from the tiny, thumb-size hemlock cone to the giant sugar pinecone that grows a foot long and often longer.

The open Virginia pinecone gives a different effect from the close-knit pitch pinecone. The tight, long, slender white fir and balsam fir cones give a sleek look to a wreath, while the wispy Douglas fir and helter-skelter white spruce cones make a wreath more playful.

Nuts, too, come in an array of shapes and sizes to give a wreath added interest. Acorns, chestnuts, pecans, almonds, and walnuts are all good to use and readily available.

Cones can be purchased at some large craft stores or found on the ground in the woods.

To prepare cones that you pick up from the woods, you must first clean them before using them for wreaths. Swirl the cones in a bucket of water to remove any sand, dirt, and bugs.

To eliminate any resin in the cones, place them on a baking sheet lined with foil and bake them in an oven set at 200 degrees Fahrenheit for 30 minutes. The resin will melt off. An alternate method is to place the cones in your refrigerator freezer for a few hours or overnight. Remove them and scrape the resin off.

Nuts in the shell also can be baked in an oven at 200 degrees for half an hour. This kills whatever insects may be inside the nuts.

Cones are simple to wire to an evergreen wreath. Florist wire can be slipped around and inside the cone and then tied to an evergreen branch.

For wreaths made entirely of cones and nuts, a solid material such as pressed artificial wood, thin plywood, or cardboard cut to a wreath shape is effective. A double-ring mold works well also, and cone wreaths have been made also with metal coat hangers twisted into circles.

To attach the cones, simply wire or glue them to the mold. For some of the smaller cones, such as from hemlocks, gluing them in place is better.

If you cut a cone in several sections horizontally, you'll create a pinecone "flower" that gives a jaunty dimension to a wreath.

The careful layering of the branches of this wreath results in an even, graceful edge. The artificial crab apples add the finishing touch — not too big, not too small. And, of course, an evergreen wreath wouldn't be complete without a big bright red ribbon.

This was placed on the front of a garage, where it made a striking picture of hospitality in an unlikely spot.

The December holidays are complete only with snow on an evergreen wreath, such as this one. Add half a dozen pinecones and a dangling red ribbon, and the homey comfort of Christmas is captured for all.

This wreath is similar to the one pictured being made on pages 35–36. The few accessories bring out the best of it. Then, when it is hung against the chocolate brown house at the beginning of a brick walkway to the front porch, the wreath turns into a welcome sign without any words.

If you have no snow from the sky to color your wreath, try some from a spray can. Except for the pinecones, this wreath is made entirely from artificial materials.

The plastic needles are sprayed with artificial snow. Then the cones and ribbon-covered balls, representing Christmas tree bulbs or winter red apples, are wired in place. Last comes the red ribbon bow, which gives the wreath a "gift present" quality.

This evergreen wreath and the next two show how small variations can change an entire tone. The evergreen bases are similar on all three, but their decorations are arranged differently.

This one has a clever, light touch of silver-white paint brushed onto the outer edges of the pinecones. The lightness of the white is just enough to draw extra attention to the wreath and hurries the eye along the evergreen circle. Small bunches of crab-apple berries break up the circle of cones and "snow," and they also set off the large panel of ribbon.

The choice of a muted, feltlike ribbon instead of a shiny satiny one keeps the overall tone underplayed but still bright.

As in the previous wreath, this one uses similar evergreen background, cones, and artificial red berries, but the ornaments are placed differently.

With the cones left unpainted, a more subdued wreath is created. But not too subdued. For example, if the red berries were removed from the center of the cone groupings, the total effect would be too dark and serious. This wreath is a good lesson in how the addition of small spots of color can generate so much beyond their size.

The ribbon has extra-long ends, too. This helps brighten the unusually dark evergreens. Yet without those tiny spots of red in the center of the cones, the ribbon would cut the wreath in half with its brightness.

This wreath is simplicity itself. Large and unmistakable, the evergreens dominate. The red berries, ribbon, cones, and baby's breath are needed, but the greenness of hope-inspiring spring is the message here.

49

The sprightliness of this wreath catches the eye with its jovial mixture of the natural and the artificial — pinecones, plastic leaves, fresh evergreens, artificial fruit.

This is the kind of wreath that makes you remember the zest and harvest of spring and summer with all its apples, peaches, and grapes.

The wreath hangs on an outside glass storm door that reflects the snow on the front lawn, making the wreath appear to be floating — wistfully — in white winter.

This wreath, too, is a mixture of natural and artificial materials. What gives it, small as it is, such movement is the circular outline of the dried field grass that fans around the entire edge.

Centered over the front door brass knocker, the wreath is positioned cleverly so that the knocker becomes part of the welcoming display.

This sunburst wreath made of cones and nuts has a beguiling symmetry to it. After the inside row of cones is wired on, it is spray painted with gold. Then the long narrow cones are attached in a vertical, outward position, giving the wreath an expansive, warm, friendly feel to it.

Leaving the outer cones to their natural shade maintains a color harmony. If all the cones were painted gold, it would be too heavy with color.

The gold-painted section includes some cones that are cut horizontally in half for a "flower" effect.

This compact wreath is appealing for its many shapes and textures. A variety of cones is included, which is its attraction. A bit of paint brushed on a few of the cones adds subtle differences and interest.

Notice how the wreath is divided into three sections by the long, narrow cones angling outward — two at the bottom, one at the upper right.

This carefully constructed wreath is based on the sunburst effect. It offers us an intriguing spectrum of textures by including some nuts, grasses, and seedpods.

Two of the cones are lightly dabbed with silver paint. While the lines of the wreath point outward like arrows, the inner section contains more circles and ovals. The two shapes blend into a pleasing balance.

This is an example, too, of a distinctive way to mount a wreath. The entire door is covered with red foil paper, setting the wreath off for special notice.

Complex yet unified by its careful arrangement, this attractive wreath is more than twenty years old. With proper care, cone-and-nut wreaths can last a generation.

The cones are wired to a simple wire base. A few artificial fruits are scattered throughout to give a mixture of color and texture; some cones are lightly painted. The original colors were brighter, but age has mellowed them to a handsome effect.

Decorations for your front door can take other shapes than the traditional circular wreath. This simple arrangement is appealing for its diagonal lines, its muted, complementary colors, and the imaginative use of natural materials.

The darkish green of the evergreens mesh to the center with delicate green and yellow tansy. The trio of cones crowns it all.

Virtually anything in a circle can be made into a wreath. This is an old spinning wheel that is wrapped with mountain laurel leaves to wonderful effect. It hangs on an outside house wall under a big front porch.

While some wreathmakers insist on using all natural materials, others use all artificial ingredients, as in this one. Made of many examples of artificial fruits, the grapes are used to give it unity. The four sets of red grapes at the top and bottom are set off by the two sets of green grapes in the middle. This cheery wreath is perfect for greetings all year round.

Here's a fine example of an imaginative wreath. Tiny presents wrapped with patience and care are glued onto a backing of cardboard (which is dressed up with a stick-on patterned paper). This fanciful mosaic of miniature presents shaped into an innovative wreath makes the eye stop and marvel at all the charming complexity. Tiny cones, little twigs, miniature porcelain figurines, and lilliputian gift boxes make an enchanting, delightful display.

6

Cloth Wreaths

CLOTH wreaths offer endless possibilities for colors, patterns, and shapes. They can be stuffed with old rags or straw, but for smoother surfaces, polyester fiber is easier to mold. It is also nonallergenic.

If you're at all handy with scissors, needle, and thread, cloth wreaths can give you a chance to put your individual creativity to work.

To make the two starburst wreaths on pages 73 and 75, cut out a circle of paper about fifteen inches in diameter. Pencil in a series of

17

18

starbursts around the pattern circle (illus. 17) and then cut out the individual triangles.

Place these paper patterns over the material to which you wish them to correspond and cut the material (illus. 18). Use three similarly patterned materials that are colored differently.

Place the triangles of material in a wreathlike circle. Work with the pieces so that you have six starbursts by positioning two triangles pointed in the same direction and then a third in the opposite direction. Keep repeating until you have your pattern set (illus. 19).

Sew the triangles together. Then cut out backing cloth and sew this to the back of the triangles. Leave two or three openings through which to stuff the wreath with polyester fiber (illus. 20).

Now sew the wreath completely shut, add a bow or ribbon of your choice, and attach a string of heavy-duty thread at the top from which to hang the wreath.

An advantage of cloth wreaths is that they can last for decades with no visible aging. Most of them are washable, too.

19   20

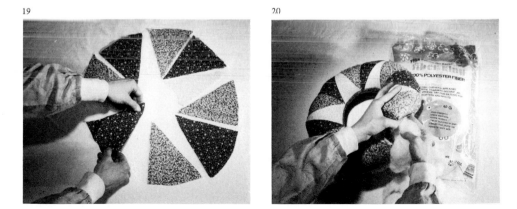

This is another example of the starburst pattern, which people find so welcoming. By using two relatively dark triangles framed against a single light one, the pattern becomes a familiar, likable image.

The bow is made of dark green, similar to the color of one of the triangles, giving the wreath a feeling of unity.

This starburst pattern shows how a simple change of colors — and a different door color — alters the effect. This wreath also has a color of bow related to one of the darker triangles. A bow the color of the starburst part of the wreath would dilute the effect.

The backing of this engaging wreath is made of the same reddish tone of one of the triangles and nicely outlines the inside of the center.

This quiltlike wreath is made with the green and red colors of Christmas and may appear uncoordinated and random on first sight — but isn't really. The wreath has eight definite sections joined together. Each of the sections is divided in two with a thin red strip down the center. In addition, each of the sections is divided into two colors. All these divisions are held together by the choice of related colors — shades of red and green — although the patterns are different. The color schemes match in opposite directions — almost. Too much symmetry here would ruin the design.

Simplicity with a twist. Three ropes filled with polyester fiber are braided and then tied end to end. Using the same checkerboard pattern for all three sections gives a clean boldness to the wreath. The ribbon hides the place where the braid was joined in a circle.

The base for this is merely a metal clothes hanger twisted into a circle. The cloth braid is tied to it from the back by white thread.

Here's an unusual example of a braided wreath. Each rope is made with different material, creating a singular effect. The wreath is loosely braided and hung with a piece of red yarn designed to be seen. The choice of the ribbon color is ideal. If the traditional bright red ribbon were attached, it would join forces with the red section of the braid and tilt the tone of the wreath out of kilter.

This endearing wreath is made from felt "seconds" that had factory defects. The maker cut around the mars, putting bad material to good use.

To make this design, first draw leaf and flower patterns on paper, cut them out, and use them to cut out the felt counterparts. Then use a felt backing to attach the parts of the visible wreath. These parts, along with sequins, are held in place with pins, some of which have fancy shiny heads deliberately placed to be seen as glitter.

This is a thin wreath that can hang just about anywhere. The possibilities for colors and fanciful shapes are open-ended.

Grapevine Wreaths and Door Decorations

Wild grapes were so widespread in early America that the first explorers called their discovery Vineland. Vines strung themselves all over the woodlands, and huge bunches of purple, white, and green grapes hung from their stems.

Today wild grapes still abound, and none of them is poisonous. In the fall, when the grapevines grow dormant for the winter, the vines lose their leaves and turn brown. This is the time to cut down sections of the vines and to form them into wreaths.

You can leave on some of the tendrils and dried grapes or strip the vines bare, depending on the effect you wish to achieve.

The plainness of this first example of a grapevine wreath has a special appeal when it is set against an old-style door. The brown tone of the simple ribbon matches the vine.

Some people shape grapevines by twisting the vine in and out of itself so that it holds by its own shape and pressure. This is better done with the thicker wreaths. Thinner wreaths may need to have the vine held together with thread or wire. Grapevine wreaths usually don't need hooks added. They're rigid and protruding enough to hang directly onto a nail.

This muted grapevine wreath has an art-ful combination of fall maple leaves and dark ribbon. Set against the white door, it presents a warm invitation that coincides with the warm colors of autumn.

A wreath like this can include some other shapes for added interest: the prickly fruit from the sycamore or sweet-gum trees, dried grapes, acorns, or winged maple seeds are good possibilities.

Small and quickly made, this wreath is a pleasant reminder of autumn. It is hung next to the front door to take advantage of the blue house paint as a background, which sends the message of the wreath clear and far.

The bright orange and red of the bitter-sweet fruit is woven around the grapevine, which is itself woven together first.

Instead of employing a ribbon or fruited plant, this wreath uses a different tact for its individuality — Indian corn. Grapevine wreaths and hard fall corn together double the symbols of the season. Actually, this wreath is made of two separate pieces. The grapevine is woven first and then placed over the corn drier, which is nailed independently to an old barn door, where it is displayed to passersby.

A corn drier is an old-time way of preparing fall corn. The tool is one piece of iron with five sharp spokes angled outward on both sides. The corn is pushed onto these spokes, and the entire piece is hung up in the air to dry the cobs.

Even if you do not own a corn drier, you can still use this form of wreath by substituting other interesting items for the drier and corn.

This wreath was made to deliberately match the color of the door. Shades of blue placed with an aesthetic sense of balance take the complicated in-and-out twists of the grapevine beyond itself. This is a grapevine wreath that, because it doesn't use only the fall colors, can remain throughout the year as an elegant greeting.

The large, dark blue petals are silk flowers; the smaller, bluish leaves are eucalyptus. The triangle of ribbons gives the wreath both brightness and symmetry.

Door decorations can take different forms from the traditional wreath. This bundle of Indian corn evokes the fall season as strongly as an evergreen wreath with a big red ribbon. With the dried corn husks bunched at the top and skirting the colorful corn itself, this is a most cordial greeting to friend and stranger alike. The subdued fall-color ribbon adds just enough notice, fitting the tone of the decoration as well as the door.

While the previous example of a door decoration signals its message with a restrained, complementary color background, this one uses contrast. This style of "broom" or "brush" is made from dried field grasses such as wheat and rye and can be decorated with a number of accessories — corn husks, dried flowers, or as in this case, oak leaves. A long, trailing ribbon that blows in the breeze adds the final touch.

One of the simplest wreathlike decorations for a door is a hat. Bright and saucy, this hat is pinned to a screen door and set off by the darkened enclosed porch inside. The long, flowing ribbon wafting in the wind keeps the decoration active, not unlike a mobile.

Any straw summer hat, with or without ribbons, can be tacked to a door as a symbol of hospitality — signaling that you can come in and doff your own hat.

The clean lines of this hanging ornament show what can be done with a few basic materials — reed mat, ribbon, cones, leaves, and needles. A light spray of white paint touches the needles with a snowlike mist. Everything is understated here, and yet this unusual — almost unlikely — wreath conveys its seasonal meaning clearly and unmistakenly.

Edible Wreaths

Making wreaths with food is an enjoyable way to draw smiles from friends and family. These wreaths provide a special treat as centerpieces for dinner tables. They also draw some surprise glances if they're hung on walls.

The wreath here has a built-in invitation to partake — scissors. This wreath is made by tying two rows of wrapped hard candy to a frame. The strings for tying are alternating red and green gift wrapping ribbons. Scissors are attached with the same type of ribbon so that passersby can cut off a candy or two, which is exactly what happened to this wreath at the Peterborough (N.H.) Public Library.

As you see in this chapter, wreaths can be made from candy, chili peppers, spices, and bread. Besides these, you might try a wreath of chocolate kisses glued to a paper-covered Styrofoam mold; or try a wreath of all nuts in the shell — walnuts, almonds, pecans, hazelnuts, and Brazil nuts. And what could be more appropriate for a kitchen wall than a wreath of herbs — sage, parsley, oregano, rosemary, tarragon, chives, and dill?

Some home gardeners braid their own garlic and onions on twine and hang them straight down for easy storage. If you form these braids into a circle and attach a ribbon, you have an edible wreath!

Although technically edible, this wreath is cooler to look at than eat. These red-hot chili peppers make an intriguing shiny wreath on a wall but are blowtorch fiery on the tongue. Foods such as these peppers can be strung by needle and thread and then tied end to end into a wreath.

Cinnamon sticks glued, layered, and then rounded into a wreath are an appetizing sight to see in any kitchen. Large cinnamon sticks like these can be found at natural foods stores or at better quality supermarkets. Other possibilities include using whole nutmegs in a wreath, or mixing the nutmegs with the cinnamon sticks.

Here's a colorful, wonderfully edible wreath. Made of soft, sugared candy, this can be a delightful centerpiece — or add a hook and hang it on a wall.

Use a Styrofoam circle wrapped with red tissue paper for the base, and stick the candies into it with toothpicks. Children especially enjoy this wreath and can have fun making it themselves.

Bread and wreaths are both ancient symbols. You can make them into a joint — and delicious — treat for everyone.

You may want to add other ingredients, such as chopped dried apricots or slivered candied orange peel, to this basic recipe:

Wreath Bread

1/2 cup raisins
1/4 cup rum (water can be substituted)
2 tablespoons dry yeast
1/2 cup warm water
1 cup water
1 tablespoon salt
1/4 cup melted sweet butter
2 extra large eggs, slightly beaten
1/4 cup sugar
2 teaspoons anise seeds
5 to 6 cups unbleached all-purpose flour
1 egg mixed with 1 teaspoon water for glaze
1/4 cup slivered almonds

1. Plump the raisins in the rum (or 1/4 cup of water) by boiling for 5 minutes.
2. Dissolve the yeast in 1/2 cup warm water in a large mixing bowl.
3. To the yeast, add 1 cup more water, then the salt, butter, 2 slightly beaten eggs, sugar, and anise seeds. Also add the plumped raisins.
4. Beat in 3 cups of the flour. Stir in 2 cups more flour. Turn out onto flat surface.
5. Knead for 8 to 10 minutes, adding flour, as needed, to prevent sticking.
6. Place in a bowl coated with vegetable oil, cover with a damp cloth, and let rise until double in bulk (about 1 1/2 hours).
7. Punch down and place on a flat surface. Form into a log shape. Cut into 3 equal pieces.
8. With your hands, roll and stretch each piece into a "rope" 36 inches long (it will be very thin).
9. Place the ropes side by side and braid them, alternating placing each outside rope between the other two. Keep the braid uniform in shape.
10. Place onto a baking sheet lightly coated with vegetable oil and sprinkled with cornmeal. Turn the braid into a wreath shape and press the ends together to seal. Cover and let rise until double in bulk (about 30 to 45 minutes).
11. Brush on the 1 egg mixed with 1 teaspoon water. Press on the slivered almonds.
12. Bake at 400 degrees F. for 25 minutes or until done. Makes 1 wreath.

Supplies

Single- and double-ring molds and coated wire and tape are available at craft and florist shops. Standard household tools such as wire cutters and pliers are found at hardware and home center stores.

Seeds from which to grow your own flowers for drying can be purchased from many large, nationally distributed seed and plant companies. One example is the Park Seed Co., Hwy. 254 N., Greenwood, SC 29647. Full color catalogs are available on request from such companies.

Smaller businesses can specialize more in flowers and plants for wreath making. Check the telephone Yellow Pages under "Artificial Flowers." Two such businesses are:

Windcrest Farm
RFD 1, Box 1420
Poor Farm Road
South Weare, NH 03281

Green Meadows Farm
Bible Hill Road
Francestown, NH 03043

Index

Achillea, 22, 24, 28
Advent, 4
Amaranth, 24
Ammobium, 26
Ankh, 1
Aphrodite, 2
Apollo, 3
Arabic countries, 2
Artemisia, 11, 13, 14–15, 16, 17,
    19, 20, 22, 26, 28
Artificial fruit, 50, 60, 66
Athens, 3

Baby's breath, 30
Balsam, 4, 5, 34
Bases 11–12
    plants for, 13
Bittersweet, 12, 88
Bridal wreaths, 2

China, 2
Chinese lantern, 26, 32
Christmas, 4, 6, 34, 40, 42
Church, the, 4
Cloth wreaths, 5, 70–71

Clothes hanger, 8, 20, 37, 78
Coffin, 2
Cone wreaths, 5, 36–37
    "flower" effect, 54
    preparation, 37
Corinth, 3
Corona convivalis, 2
Corona funebris, 2
Crowns, 3, 4

Della Robbia, 4
Delphi, 3
Delphinium, 24, 28
Design, 17–18
Display, 1–2, 5–7
Dried flowers, 4, 5, 6
    drying, 12–13, 20

Easter, 6
Egypt, 1
Eucalyptus, 24, 92
Evergreen wreaths, 4, 5, 6
    preparing, 34–36

Felt wreath, 82–83
Fillet, woolen, 3

Glue gun, 8, 17
Goldenrod, 24
Grapevines, 12, 85
Grasses, 24, 52, 96
Greece, 2-3
Green Meadows Farm, 113

Halos, 4
Hat wreath, 98
Hera, 2
Herb wreaths, 7, 14, 103
Herbs, 5
Hymen, 2

Indian corn, 90, 94
Isthmian Games, 3
Italy, 4

Jesus, 3
Jewish Feast of the Tabernacle, 2

Laurel, 3, 4

Marriage ceremony, 2
Materials, 8–9
Molds
    hemp, 17
    ring, 15
    straw, 16, 19
Moth preventative (santolina), 14

Nemean Games, 3
New Year's Day, 6
Nuts, 36, 37

Oak leaves, 3, 4
Olympic Games, 3
Oregano, 30

Park Seed Co., 113
Polyester fiber, 70, 71, 78
Presents (wreath), 68
Principles (guidelines), 10-11
Pythian Games, 3

Recipe, wreath bread, 110
Reed mat, 100
Ring molds, 11, 15, 34–36
Romans, 3
Royalty, 4

Silica gel, 12, 20
Silk flowers, 92
Spanish moss, 10, 13, 15
Spinning wheel, 64
Spray, 18
Statice, 26
Straw flowers, 26, 32
Styrofoam, 12, 103, 108
Sweet William, 28
Symbols, 1, 2, 4

Thanksgiving, 6
Tools, 8–9, 16–17

Valentine wreath, 30

Windcrest Farm, 113
Wreaths
    advent, 4
    bread, 110
    bridal, 2
    cone, 36–37
    display of, 1–2
    dried-flower, 4
    Easter, 6
    edible, 103–111
    evergreen, 4, 34–36
    felt, 82
    grapevine, 85
    hat, 98
    herb, 7, 13, 103
    history of, 1–4
    laurel, 3
    oak, 3, 4
    presents, 68
    reed, 100
    symbols, 1, 2, 6
    Valentine, 30